the TechnoLogy beHIND

EVERYDAY APPLIANCES

Nicolas Brasch

- ➲ What Makes a Lightbulb Light Up?
- ➲ How Does a Zipper Work?
- ➲ What Keeps Nonstick Frying Pans from Sticking?

Smart Apple Media
P.O. Box 3263
Mankato, MN, 56002

First published in 2010 by
MACMILLAN EDUCATION AUSTRALIA PTY LTD
15–19 Claremont St, South Yarra, Australia 3141

Visit our web site at www.macmillan.com.au or go directly to www.macmillanlibrary.com.au

Associated companies and representatives throughout the world.

Library of Congress Cataloging-in-Publication Data

Brasch, Nicolas.
   Everyday appliances / Nicolas Brasch.
      p. cm. — (The technology behind)
   Includes bibliographical references and index.
   ISBN 978-1-59920-566-3 (library bound)
   1. Technology—Juvenile literature. 2. Technological innovations—Juvenile literature. I. Title.
   T48.B782 2011
600—dc22

                                                                                    2009054433

Publisher: Carmel Heron
Managing Editor: Vanessa Lanaway
Editor: Georgina Garner
Proofreader: Erin Richards
Designer: Stella Vassiliou
Page layout: Stella Vassiliou and Raul Diche
Photo researcher: Wendy Duncan (management: Debbie Gallagher)
Illustrators: Alan Laver, pp. 7, 8, 9, 10, 11, 12, 13, 15, 17, 19, 20, 21, 23, 25, 26, 27, 28, 29;
   Richard Morden, p. 6; Karen Young, p. 1 and Try This! logo.
Production Controller: Vanessa Johnson

Manufactured in China by Macmillan Production (Asia) Ltd.
Kwun Tong, Kowloon, Hong Kong
Supplier Code: CP March 2010

Acknowledgements

The author and the publisher are grateful to the following for permission to reproduce copyright material:

Front cover photographs:
Zipper © Shutterstock/Denis and Yulia Pogostins; Egg © Shutterstock/carroteater; Television © Jupiter Images Unlimited/Bananastock.

© Bettmann/Corbis, **11**, **16** (top); © Hulton-Deutsch Collection/Corbis, **16** (bottom); © Radius/Corbis, **18** (bottom); © Ramin Talaie/Corbis, **31** (left); © RCWW, Inc./Corbis, **31** (center); © Dreamstime/Mikhail Basov, **5** (center); © Dreamstime/Peter Gudella, **5** (bottom); © Image Source/Getty Images, **30**; © Gerry Wade/ Taxi/Getty Images, **5** (top); Courtesy of the Hagley Museum and Library (HF_T022_003), **22** (bottom); www.inventors.about.com, **5**; © Özgür Donmaz/iStockphoto, **18** (center); © Wendell Franks/iStockphoto, **20**; © Jim Jurica/iStockphoto, **6** (left); © Matej Pribelsky/iStockphoto, **22** (top); © Chris Schmidt/ iStockphoto, **4**; © Jupiter Images/Foodpix/Getty Images, **28**; © Jupiter Images Unlimited/Bananastock, **25**; National Anthropological Archives, Smithsonian Institution 211195/08575700, **14** (right); photolibrary/ Alamy/Image Farm Inc., **7**; photolibrary/Alamy/Rieke Hammerich, **14** (left); © Shutterstock/Borodaev, **6** (right); © Shutterstock/Natalia Bratslavsky, **18** (top).

While every care has been taken to trace and acknowledge copyright, the publisher tenders their apologies for any accidental infringement where copyright has proved untraceable. Where the attempt has been unsuccessful, the publisher welcomes information that would redress the situation.

The publisher would like to thank Heidi Ruhnau, Head of Science at Oxley College, for her assistance in reviewing manuscripts.

Please note

At the time of printing, the Internet addresses appearing in this book were correct. Owing to the dynamic nature of the Internet, however, we cannot guarantee that all these addresses will remain correct.

▶ Contents

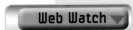

Look out for these features throughout the book:

"Word Watch" explains the meanings of words shown in **bold**

"Web Watch" provides web site suggestions for further research

What Is Technology?

The First Tools
One of the first examples of technology, where humans used their knowledge of the world to their advantage, was when humans began shaping and carving stone and metals into tools such as axes and chisels.

▲ People use technology every day, such as when they turn on computers. Technology is science put into action to help humans and solve problems.

Technology is the use of **science** for practical purposes, such as building bridges, inventing machines, and improving materials. Humans have been using technology since they built the first shelters and lit the first fires.

Technology in People's Lives

Technology is behind many things in people's everyday lives, from lightbulbs to can openers. It has shaped the sports shoes people wear and helped them run faster. Cars, trains, airplanes, and space shuttles are all products of technology. Engineers use technology to design and construct materials and structures such as bridges, roads, and buildings. Technology can be seen in amazing built structures all around humans.

Technology is responsible for how people communicate with each other. Information technology uses scientific knowledge to determine ways to spread information widely and quickly. Recently, this has involved the creation of the Internet, and e-mail and file-sharing technologies. In the future, technology may become even more a part of people's lives, with the development of robots and artificial intelligence for use in business, in the home, and in science.

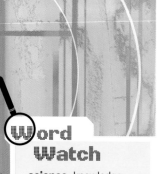

Word Watch

science knowledge that humans have gathered about the physical and natural world and how it works

The Technology Behind Everyday Appliances

At home, at school, and in offices, people are surrounded by **devices** and products that make life easier, more productive, and more entertaining. All these everyday appliances have one thing in common: we cannot imagine how people lived without them.

New Inventions

Some everyday appliances, such as the screw and the steam iron, are the result of scientific discoveries and gradual changes in technology over hundreds of years. Others, such as Post-it® Notes, seemed to spring up out of nowhere.

Some appliances are invented because there is a need for them, such as can openers. Other appliances help us do the same things but in a new way, such as using a zipper to fasten our jeans instead of buttons.

Most Popular Inventions

Of all the things that have been invented, humans seem to value everyday appliances the most. According to a web site, the 10 most popular inventions are:

- telephone
- computer
- television
- automobile
- cotton gin (a machine that separates cotton after it has been picked)
- camera
- steam engine
- sewing machine
- lightbulb
- penicillin

Source: www.inventors.about.com

▲ Computer

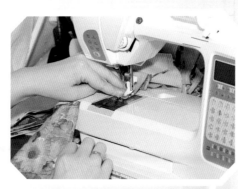
▲ Sewing machine

▲ Lightbulb

Word Watch

devices things made for a particular purpose or to do a particular job

industrial to do with activities concerned with making goods to sell, often in factories

How Does a Screw Work?

One of the most common objects in homes, offices, schools, and other buildings is a tiny metal **device** that is normally hidden from view. Screws can be found just about everywhere—inside computers and cupboards, in tables and chairs, and on door frames and windowsills.

A Screw

A screw is usually used to join two materials together. When turned one way, a screw moves farther and farther into a material. The screw cannot be pulled out because of **friction** between the screw and the material. If turned in the opposite direction, however, the screw will move farther and farther out of the material.

History of the Screw

The screw shape was first used as a device for raising water out of a river or well. This technique was used in the Middle East from about 700 B.C., and it was described by the Greek scientist Archimedes in about 250 B.C. The device became known as an Archimedes's screw.

It was not until the 1400s in Europe that the screw began to be used as a **fastener**. Fastening screws were handmade until the late 1700s when British instrument maker Jesse Ramsden invented a **lathe** for making screws. The screws had a single groove across the top.

▲ The double-grooved Phillips head screw was invented in 1936.

▲ The Archimedes's screw was controlled by a handle and positioned within a hollow pipe or tube. As it turned, it carried water up the hollow pipe. This kind of screw could also be used to press wine and olives.

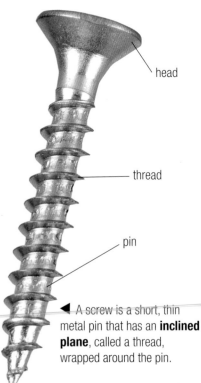

head

thread

pin

◀ A screw is a short, thin metal pin that has an **inclined plane**, called a thread, wrapped around the pin.

A Screwdriver

A screwdriver is a tool for inserting, securing, and removing screws. It has a metal shaft, at the end of which is a tip that fits into the groove or grooves on the head of a screw. Screwdrivers that have a single edge are for screws with a single groove. Other screwdrivers have tips with multiple edges or patterned imprints to fit particular types of screws. The handle of a screwdriver is designed to fit neatly in a person's hand.

▶ The technology behind the screwdriver lies in the turning **force**, called torque, and the large size of the screwdriver's handle compared to the small size of the screw.

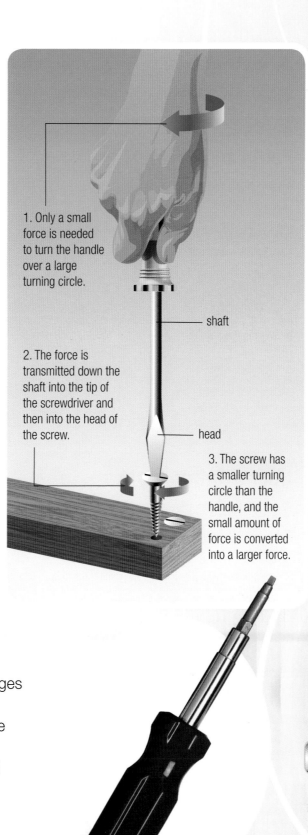

1. Only a small force is needed to turn the handle over a large turning circle.

shaft

2. The force is transmitted down the shaft into the tip of the screwdriver and then into the head of the screw.

head

3. The screw has a smaller turning circle than the handle, and the small amount of force is converted into a larger force.

History of the Screwdriver

The screwdriver was invented in Europe in the 1700s, probably in France. It had several design changes throughout the 1800s, but then remained fairly unchanged for more than 100 years. In the 1900s, the Robertson and Phillips screws and screwdrivers were designed.

▶ The Robertson screwdriver was invented in 1908. The screwdriver has a square tip.

European Invention
The screwdriver is one of the few tools that was invented in Europe without a similar device being invented by the Chinese.

Direction of the Thread
Most screws have a right-hand thread, and the screwdriver should be turned clockwise to tighten the screw and counterclockwise to loosen it. A left-hand screw is only used where a right-hand screw might become loosened due to lots of counterclockwise movement, such as for the screw on the left-hand pedal of a bike.

Word Watch

force a push or a pull

Web Watch ▼

www.sciencetech.
technomuses.ca/english/
schoolzone/Info_Simple_
Machines2.cfm#screw

home.howstuffworks.com/
screwdriver.htm

What Is a Toilet's S-bend?

We use toilets every day but most of us have no idea how they work—although we are very pleased that they work so well. The S-bend is the part of a toilet that makes sure that what goes down a toilet doesn't come back up!

Parts of a Toilet

The bowl, siphon, and tank are the three main parts of the toilet. Both the bowl and the tank have water in them.

▶ Most toilets have the same basic parts.

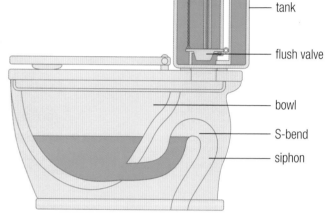

refill valve
float
overflow tube
tank
flush valve
bowl
S-bend
siphon

How a Toilet Works

A toilet flushes human waste away.

1 » When a person wants to flush a toilet, he or she pushes a button or handle. This pulls a chain in the tank that releases the flush valve, which floats up and exposes a hole.

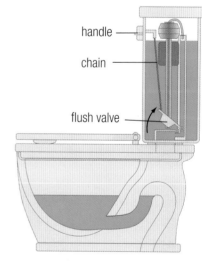

handle
chain
flush valve

2 » Water flows through the exposed hole from the tank into the bowl. This raises the level of the water in the bowl until it reaches the top of the S-bend in the siphon. Water and waste from the bowl flows down the siphon and into the sewer pipes.

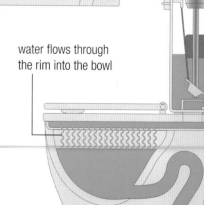

water flows through the rim into the bowl

Try This!

Flushing Without Pressing A Button

If the button on your toilet is broken and the flush will not work, you can still flush the toilet. Just fill a bucket with water and pour the water into the toilet bowl. The extra water causes the water level to rise above the top of the S-bend. When enough water has run out, the rest of the water will remain in the bowl.

3 ›› Once the tank is empty of water, the flush valve falls back into place covering the hole.

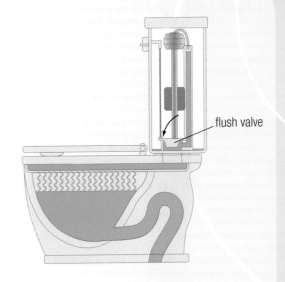

flush valve

4 ›› The float in the tank is attached to the refill valve. As the water level in the tank falls, the float also falls, turning on the refill valve, which lets fresh water into the tank. The water level rises again, and the float starts to rise, too. When the float hits the top, it turns the refill valve off, stopping any more water from entering the tank.

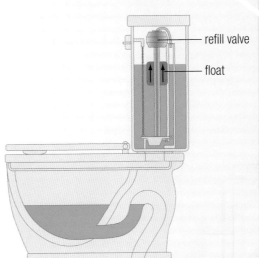

refill valve

float

Word Watch

device something made for a particular purpose or to do a particular job

5 ›› Another important **device** in the tank is the overflow tube. If the refill valve does not turn off, water continues to run into the tank. If this happens, the overflow tube directs extra water back into the bowl and stops water from spilling over the top of the tank and onto the floor. Even if water keeps running into the tank and then into the bowl, the extra water will end up running through the siphon and out through the sewer pipe.

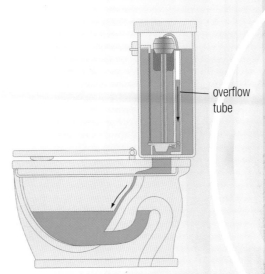

overflow tube

Web Watch

home.howstuffworks.com/ toilet.htm

Lightbulbs have been around since the 1800s, and the design of some has remained almost unchanged. With a simple flick of a switch, they light up a room! We all enjoy the technology of the lightbulb.

Incandescent Lightbulbs

Common pear-shaped lightbulbs are incandescent bulbs. These lightbulbs are very inefficient. This is because 90 percent of the energy they give out is in the form of heat and only 10 percent is in the form of light.

How an Incandescent Lightbulb Works

When a light switch is turned on, electricity enters the bulb through the contacts at its base. The electricity travels up the wires to the filament. The electricity heats the filament to the point where it glows white.

The End of the Incandescent Lightbulb?

In 2007, Australia became the first country to announce that it would ban incandescent lightbulbs to save energy. Other countries have followed.

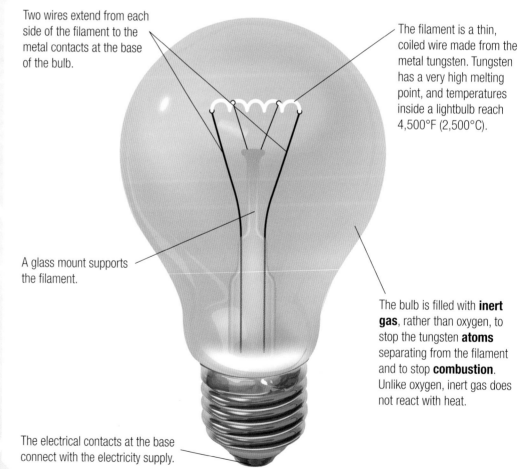

Two wires extend from each side of the filament to the metal contacts at the base of the bulb.

The filament is a thin, coiled wire made from the metal tungsten. Tungsten has a very high melting point, and temperatures inside a lightbulb reach 4,500°F (2,500°C).

A glass mount supports the filament.

The bulb is filled with **inert gas**, rather than oxygen, to stop the tungsten **atoms** separating from the filament and to stop **combustion**. Unlike oxygen, inert gas does not react with heat.

The electrical contacts at the base connect with the electricity supply.

Word Watch

atoms smallest parts of a substance

combustion process of burning

inert gas gases such as argon that do no react with other substances

▲ Incandescent means "white with heat." The filament in an incandescent lightbulb glows white hot.

Fluorescent Lightbulbs

Fluorescent bulbs are more efficient than incandescent bulbs because they produce more light per unit of electricity. They do not lose so much energy in the form of heat.

How a Fluorescent Lightbulb Works

When a fluorescent lightbulb is connected to an electricity source, the electrodes emit particles called **electrons**. These electrons travel around the tube and collide with mercury atoms. When they collide, the electrons release a burst of ultraviolet light. Ultraviolet light cannot be seen by humans, but phosphor powder turns the ultraviolet light into visible light.

▶ Thomas Edison researched and developed an incandescent lightbulb in the 1870s.

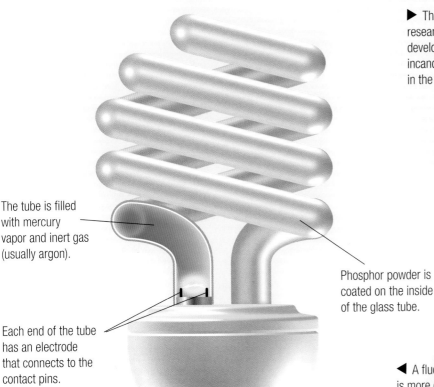

The tube is filled with mercury vapor and inert gas (usually argon).

Each end of the tube has an electrode that connects to the contact pins.

Phosphor powder is coated on the inside of the glass tube.

◀ A fluorescent lightbulb is more energy efficient than an incandescent bulb. It can last more than 10 times as long, too.

The contact pins connect with the electricity source.

The First Lightbulbs

The first public display of incandescent light came from the British scientist Humphry Davy in 1802. The first incandescent lightbulbs that could be easily produced and sold were invented by two different men in two different parts of the world during 1878–79. Those men were Joseph Swan, in England, and Thomas Edison, in the United States.

Word Watch

electrons particles that orbit the nuclei (centers) of atoms

Web Watch ▼

home.howstuffworks.com/light-bulb1.htm
home.howstuffworks.com/fluorescent-lamp.htm
videos.howstuffworks.com/science-channel/37431-deconstructed-incandescent-light-bulbs-video.htm

How Does a Zipper Work?

Without zipper technology, people would have to fiddle with buttons to do up their jeans, boots, and jackets. The simple zipper is made up of a combination of wedges and hooks.

How a Wedge Works

A wedge is an object with a slanted surface that is designed to move something apart or keep two things apart. When you apply a wedge to an object, the energy that you apply pushing the wedge in converts to a **force** that works at right angles to the wedge's movement.

▶ When a doorstop wedge is jammed under a door, the bottom of the door is forced upward. This upward movement is at right angles to the forward movement of the wedge.

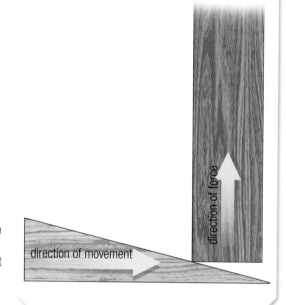

direction of force

direction of movement

Word Watch

device something made for a particular purpose or to do a particular job

fastener something that joins two things together securely

force a push or a pull

How a Hook Works

A hook is a curved piece of material that grabs onto and secures another material. It is a **fastener**. An everyday example of a hook is a curved **device** on the back of a door for hanging hats and coats. Hooks are often metal.

hook

hole for hook

◀ A door can be kept closed using a hook. The metal door hook is placed inside a circular piece of metal to fasten the door.

Web Watch
science.howstuffworks.com/zipper.htm

www.essortment.com/hobbies/howzipperswork_saoi.htm

How a Zipper Works

The wedges and hooks in a zipper work together to fasten and unfasten the zipper. The zipper's slide contains three wedges and the zipper's teeth are made up of hooks and hollows.

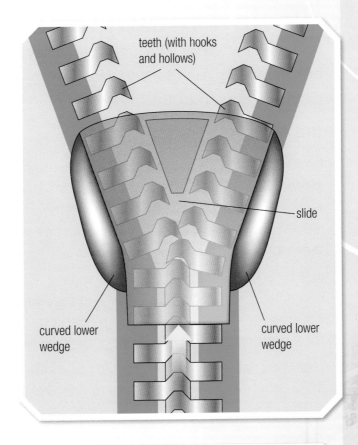

teeth (with hooks and hollows)

slide

curved lower wedge

curved lower wedge

triangular upper wedge

▶ When the slide is pulled up the zipper, the lower wedges in the slide push the hooks into hollows, securing the teeth and fastening the zipper.

▶ When the slide is pulled down the zipper, the upper wedge detaches the hooks from the hollows and forces the teeth apart, opening the zipper.

Inventing the Zipper

The zipper was invented by American engineer Whitcomb Judson in 1893. He wanted to make it easier to close and open men's boots, but his design was complicated and not practical. In 1912, Swedish engineer Gideon Sundback improved the design.

A Popular Invention

The zipper became a popular and practical device after 1912. The first large-scale use of zippers was by the US Navy, which ordered 10,000 zippers for flying suits in 1918.

Why Do You Put Water in an Iron?

A modern steam iron removes wrinkles from clothes, using both heat and moisture. Throughout history, various materials—including bronze, glass, marble, and wood—have been used to make **devices** that smooth clothes.

History of the Iron

Devices to smooth or press clothes have been used in Europe and Asia for at least 2,000 years. The ancient Romans used a device that was made up of two heavy wooden boards joined together with wooden screws. Clothes were placed between the boards and the screws were tightened as far as they would go, flattening the material.

In the 1300s, **blacksmiths** started making flat irons out of metal. These irons had a flat base like today's irons, and they were held over a fire until they became hot. Their handles were made from metal or wood, so the user held thick pads to protect his or her hands from burning.

Gas irons came into use in the 1870s, and the first electric iron was invented in 1882, but many homes were not connected to electricity at this time. The first steam iron was sold by Eldec Company, an American company, in 1926.

Ironing Boards

The first folding ironing boards appeared in the 1860s. Before then, people ironed on many different surfaces, such as wooden tables, boards made from whalebone, and boards that were balanced between two pieces of furniture.

Word Watch

blacksmiths people who make and repair things made from iron

devices things made for particular purposes or to do particular jobs

▲ Many flat irons were made out of metal. Others were made from stone or terra-cotta, which is a type of earth.

▲ The ancient Chinese created a device similar to the modern iron. It was a metal pan with an open compartment, a flat base, and a handle. Hot coals were placed in the compartment and the flat base was pressed on stretched material and clothes.

The Modern Steam Iron

The modern steam iron uses both heat and moisture to remove wrinkles from clothes. The heat and moisture create steam, which softens the fibers of the clothes, making it easier for the iron to stretch out the fibers and remove wrinkles. The handle and the entire upper part of the iron are made from plastic. Plastic does not heat up like other materials, so the person who is ironing does not burn his or her hand.

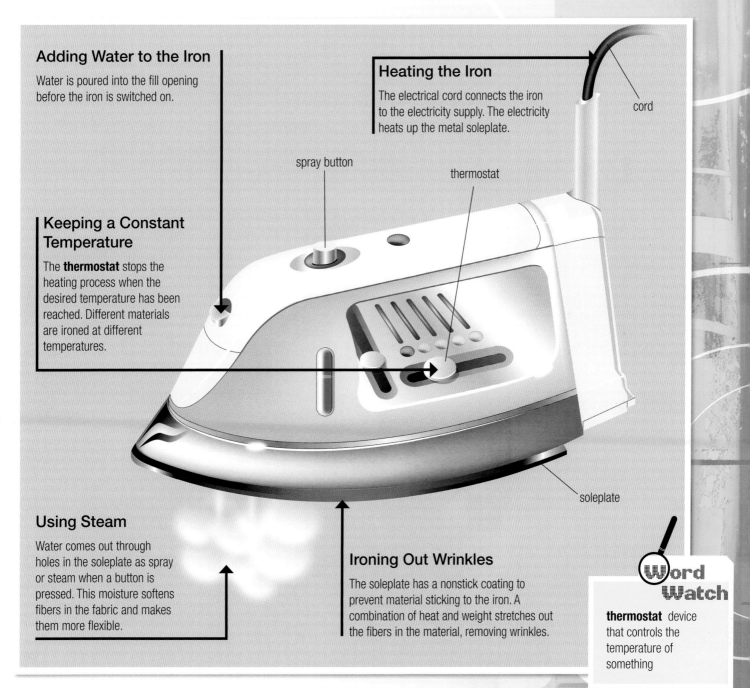

Adding Water to the Iron

Water is poured into the fill opening before the iron is switched on.

Heating the Iron

The electrical cord connects the iron to the electricity supply. The electricity heats up the metal soleplate.

cord

spray button

thermostat

Keeping a Constant Temperature

The **thermostat** stops the heating process when the desired temperature has been reached. Different materials are ironed at different temperatures.

soleplate

Using Steam

Water comes out through holes in the soleplate as spray or steam when a button is pressed. This moisture softens fibers in the fabric and makes them more flexible.

Ironing Out Wrinkles

The soleplate has a nonstick coating to prevent material sticking to the iron. A combination of heat and weight stretches out the fibers in the material, removing wrinkles.

Word Watch

thermostat device that controls the temperature of something

How Does a Refrigerator Keep Things Cold?

It might surprise you to know that cool air is not pumped into a refrigerator. Instead, hot air is drawn out of the refrigerator, which cools down the objects inside. Refrigerators work on the basis of a scientific law called the second law of thermodynamics.

History of the Refrigerator

The first refrigeration machine was invented by American Oliver Evans in 1805. This was just a model, but several other inventors began making and selling refrigeration **devices** based on Evans's invention.

The first refrigerator used for commercial purposes was designed and built by Australian James Harrison in the 1850s. It was used mostly by brewing and meat companies to keep beer and meat cold.

By the 1890s, there were a number of refrigeration devices but none were suitable—or cheap enough—for homes. Manufacturers began to realize that there was a huge market for home refrigerators. In 1911, refrigerators for the home began to be sold. The first combination fridge-and-freezers were sold in 1939.

The Second Law of Thermodynamics

This scientific law basically states that energy tends to spread out. If a hot object is placed next to a cold object, the heat energy will spread out from the hot object, so that the cold object will get warmer and the hot object will cool down. Thus, the temperature of the environment around an object will affect the temperature of that object. For example, a bowl of hot soup sitting in a cold room will cool down, while the air in the room will warm up very slightly.

◀ U.S. company General Motors produced its first Frigidaire (pictured) in 1921. By 1926, the cost of a Frigidaire had dropped by almost half due to improved technology.

◀ Since the 1950s, the refrigerator has become the most used household appliance in many countries. In some countries, more than 99 percent of homes have a refrigerator.

Thermo = Heat

Thermodynamics is the **science** that deals with the relationship between heat and other forms of energy. The name comes from the Greek word *thermo*, meaning "heat."

Word Watch

devices things made for particular purposes or to do particular jobs

science knowledge that humans have gathered about the physical and natural world and how it works

Inside a Refrigerator

Refrigeration involves a substance, called a refrigerant, traveling through pipes in different forms.

Refrigerant Gases

For many years, the gas used as a refrigerant was a chlorofluorocarbon (CFC), but this type of gas was found to harm the environment. Today, a less harmful gas called tetrafluoroethane is used.

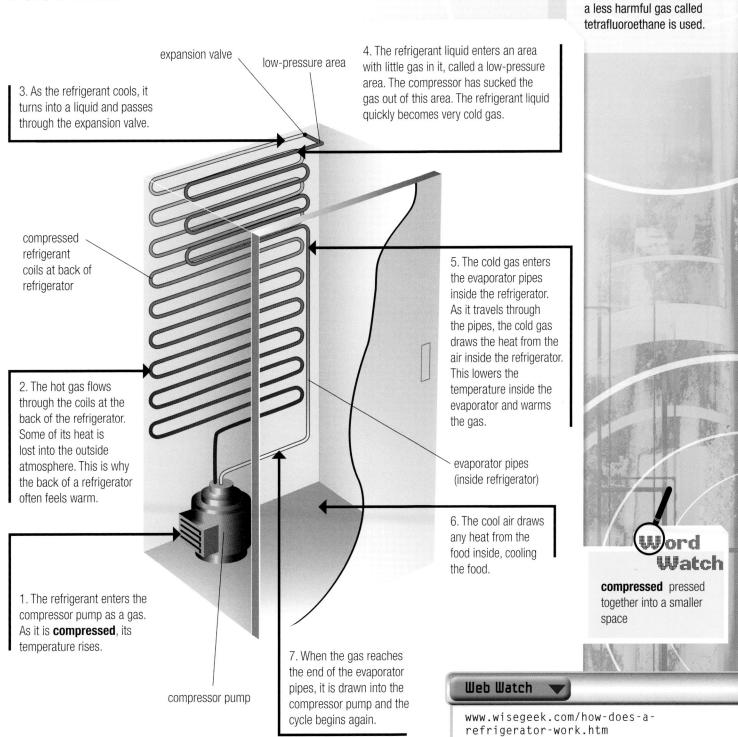

expansion valve

low-pressure area

3. As the refrigerant cools, it turns into a liquid and passes through the expansion valve.

4. The refrigerant liquid enters an area with little gas in it, called a low-pressure area. The compressor has sucked the gas out of this area. The refrigerant liquid quickly becomes very cold gas.

compressed refrigerant coils at back of refrigerator

5. The cold gas enters the evaporator pipes inside the refrigerator. As it travels through the pipes, the cold gas draws the heat from the air inside the refrigerator. This lowers the temperature inside the evaporator and warms the gas.

2. The hot gas flows through the coils at the back of the refrigerator. Some of its heat is lost into the outside atmosphere. This is why the back of a refrigerator often feels warm.

evaporator pipes (inside refrigerator)

6. The cool air draws any heat from the food inside, cooling the food.

1. The refrigerant enters the compressor pump as a gas. As it is **compressed**, its temperature rises.

compressor pump

7. When the gas reaches the end of the evaporator pipes, it is drawn into the compressor pump and the cycle begins again.

Word Watch

compressed pressed together into a smaller space

Web Watch

www.wisegeek.com/how-does-a-refrigerator-work.htm

www.howstuffworks.com/refrigerator.htm

Does a Vacuum Flask Keep Things Hot or Cold?

A vacuum flask maintains the temperature of the liquid that is placed inside it, so it can keep things either hot or cold. A vacuum flask is also known as a thermos.

How Heat Travels

Before looking at the technology behind a vacuum flask, it is necessary to understand how heat travels. Heat travels in three ways: conduction, convection, and **radiation**.

Heat Transfer and Cooking

Food can be heated and cooked using conduction, convection, or radiation. Placing a piece of meat on a hot frying pan heats the meat by conduction. Placing a piece of meat on a barbecue grill and then lighting the grill heats the meat by convection. Placing a piece of meat in a microwave oven and turning the microwave on heats the meat by radiation.

Conduction

Conduction involves the movement of heat between two objects that are touching each other. If you put your hand under hot running water, the heat from the water will warm your hands.

◄ If you place a metal teaspoon in a cup of hot coffee, heat will travel up the spoon until even the part of the spoon that is out of the liquid is very hot. This is an example of conduction.

Convection

Convection is the transfer of heat by the movement of the warmed matter. Warm liquids and gases rise, and their place is taken by cooler liquids or gases. This is how a cup of hot coffee or tea cools down. The heat rises to the top and out of the cup, until there is little heat left in the liquid.

◄ Convection is the reason that a hot-air balloon flies. A burner heats the air inside the balloon, the warm air rises, and the balloon lifts.

Radiation

Objects that are hot give off **infrared** radiation. Humans cannot see infrared radiation, but they can feel it as heat. The coals of a fire that seems to have gone out still give off energy, in the form of heat. Another example of radiation is from the sun.

◄ An open fire radiates warmth. A person can feel the heat without touching the hot fire.

Word Watch

infrared light that is too red for the eye to detect

radiation energy, such as light or heat, that travels from its source through material or space

Inside a Vacuum Flask

The design of a vacuum flask works to stop heat from being transferred through conduction, convection, or radiation. This allows hot or cold liquids to stay hot or cold for several hours. Liquids do eventually cool down or heat up, however, because a small amount of heat escapes or enters through both the cap and the top of the flask.

▼ The features of a vacuum flask help it reduce and slow the transfer of heat.

The vacuum is the space between the two layers of glass or steel. A vacuum is an area in which there are no **atoms**. Without atoms, conduction and convection cannot take place.

The outside of the flask and the cap are made from materials that are good **insulators**. This adds extra protection from loss of heat or cold.

The inner glass or steel has a reflective lining, which reflects infrared radiation back into the liquid.

Word Watch

atoms smallest parts of substances

insulators materials that slow down the transfer of heat to or from an object

Web Watch ▼

www.school-for-champions.
com/science/thermos.htm

home.howstuffworks.com/
thermos.htm

www.explainthatstuff.com/
vacuumflasks.html

How Does a Can Opener Work?

Often the invention of one **device** leads to the invention of another. Good examples are cans and can openers. Once humans discovered that metal cans could be used to preserve food, someone needed to invent a way of opening the cans easily.

Wedges and Levers

A can opener is a lever that uses a wedge. A wedge is an object with a slanted surface that is designed to move something apart (see page 12), and a lever is a device that has a **fulcrum** about which the lever turns or is supported. Levers are designed to make it easier to lift heavy objects. When effort is applied to one part of the lever, a **load** is lifted with the help of the fulcrum. There are three types of levers, called first class, second class, and third class levers. They differ according to the position of the fulcrum, effort, and load.

(see page 12)

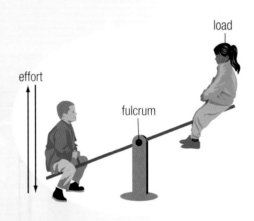

▲ First class levers have the effort on one end of the fulcrum and the load on the other end of the fulcrum. A seesaw is an example of a first class lever.

▲ Second class levers have the fulcrum at one end, the effort at the other end, and the load in the middle. A wheelbarrow is an example of a second class lever.

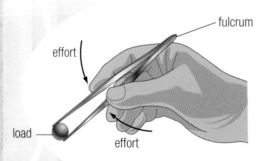

▲ Third class levers have the fulcrum at one end, the load at the other end, and the effort in the middle. A pair of tweezers is an example of a third class lever.

▲ A can opener is an example of a second class lever. The effort is placed at the end of the handles. The fulcrum is the toothed wheel of the can opener, and the load is the point where the can opener holds the can.

Much Needed Technology

Before the can opener was invented, cans of food were opened with a hammer and chisel or with any other tools that would force the can open.

Word Watch

device something made for a particular purpose or to do a particular job
fulcrum hinge or pivot
load weight to be lifted

20

Using a Can Opener

There are a few steps that are common to using all can openers.

First Can Openers
The first hand-operated can opener was invented by American Ezra Warner in 1858. The first electric can opener was invented in 1931.

1 » The user grips the handles, applying pressure and fixing the toothed wheel and blade to the top of the can. The toothed wheel grips the lower edge of the can's lip. The blade acts like a wedge and cuts into the inside of the lip of the can.

2 » The key is turned, which moves the toothed wheel.

3 » As the toothed wheel turns around and around, it turns the round blade, too. The wheel and the blade make their way around the can. The blade cuts the top of the can as it goes.

4 » Once the blade has cut all around the top of the can, the user loosens his or her grip, moves the can opener away from the open can, and removes the lid. Some can openers help lift off the lid, but others require the user to remove the lid.

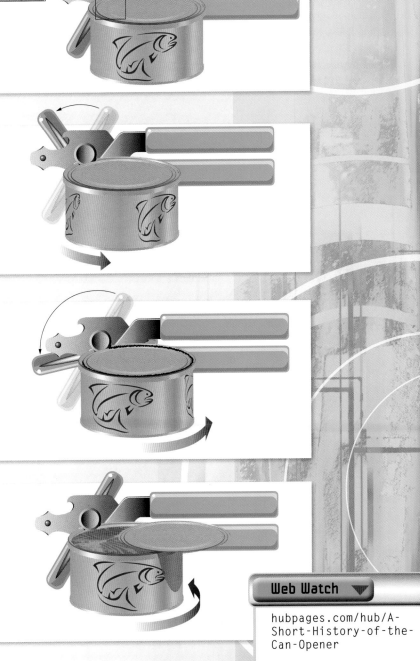

Web Watch ▼

hubpages.com/hub/A-Short-History-of-the-Can-Opener

What Keeps Nonstick Frying Pans from Sticking?

Nonstick frying pans are coated with a substance called polytetrafluoroethylene (PTFE). Polytetrafluoroethylene is thought to be the most slippery material in existence.

About PTFE

Polytetrafluoroethylene is made up of the chemicals carbon and fluorine. Together, these chemicals create a very strong **bond**. PTFE has a very high melting point of 621°F (327°C). It is very slippery so it is used as a coating in machines where **mechanical** parts rub against each other, as well as on nonstick pans.

▲ PTFE has a very high melting point, so it can be used safely on cookware such as pots and pans.

Discovery of PTFE

PTFE was accidentally discovered on April 6, 1938, in a laboratory in New Jersey. Chemist Roy Plunkett was trying to find the right combination of gases to use in refrigerators (see pages 16–17). He put one of his samples in a special container and when he checked on it later he found that it had turned into a white, waxy solid. This was polytetrafluoroethylene.

His employers recognized the nonstick qualities of PTFE and started manufacturing the substance for **industrial** purposes.

The idea of using PTFE on cookware is credited to Frenchman Marc Grégoire. In 1954, Grégoire was using PTFE on his fishing line to stop it from tangling. His wife asked if she could try it on a frying pan to see if it would stop food from sticking to the pan. The result was the world's first nonstick frying pan. Within a few years, many companies were making nonstick pans.

▲ Roy Plunkett (right) was the DuPont employee who discovered PTFE. DuPont called his discovery Teflon®.

How Does PTFE Stick to a Frying Pan?

If PTFE is so slippery and nothing can stick to it, how does PTFE stick to a frying pan? Scientists have discovered different ways to do this.

Originally, scientists **sandblasted** the frying pan to form tiny mounds and bumps. The PTFE was then poured into the pan and it stuck in the grooves and on the points of the bumps. With normal household use, however, the PTFE soon started coming loose.

Now, the sandblasted method is still used but a **primer** is applied before the PTFE is added. This primer sets in the bumps and grooves and is then baked to make sure it sticks tight. The primer contains several chemicals, including carbon and fluorine, which are in PTFE. This is the key, because there is one thing that PTFE will stick to, and that is itself. So, when PTFE is applied to the primer, some of it sticks. The baking process is then repeated to harden the whole mixture.

Geckos and PTFE

It is claimed that PTFE is the only substance that a gecko cannot stick to. Geckos have very sticky microscopic hairs on their feet, which allow them to climb walls and run across ceilings.

Word Watch

primer special substance used as a first coating

sandblasted roughen or clean a surface using a jet of sand

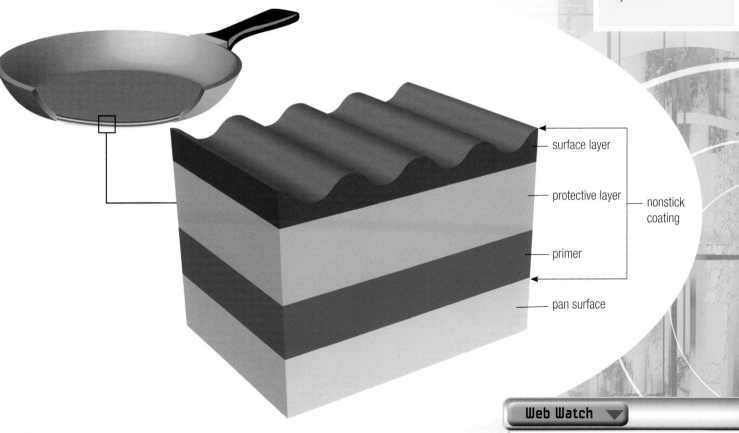

surface layer

protective layer

nonstick coating

primer

pan surface

▲ Layers of PTFE are added to a pan, building up the nonstick coating.

Web Watch ▼

www2.dupont.com/Teflon/en_US/
products/safety/what_is_it.html

How Does a Television Signal Travel Through the Air?

Television signals that travel through the air are actually made up of two signals—sound and light. Understanding how these signals travel from a television studio to your home requires an understanding of how sound and light travel.

Waves That Travel Through the Air

Sound and light can travel through the air in waves. These waves are measured by their length and **frequency**.

Light waves are part of the electromagnetic spectrum. The electromagnetic spectrum is made up of all the **rays** and waves that travel through the air. Sound is not an electromagnetic wave, but it can be carried on radio waves.

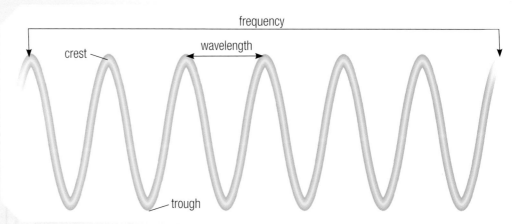

▲ The bottom of a wave is called the trough. The top of a wave is called the crest. The length of a wave is measured from one crest to the next crest or from one trough to the next trough.

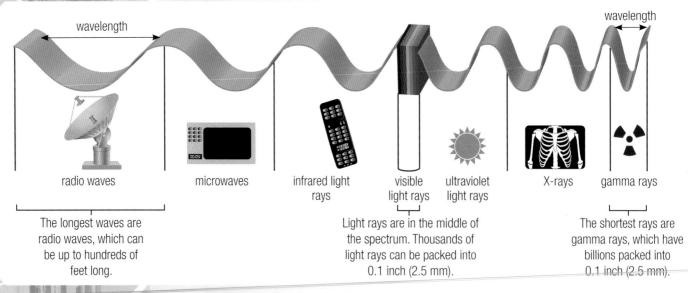

radio waves   microwaves   infrared light rays   visible light rays   ultraviolet light rays   X-rays   gamma rays

The longest waves are radio waves, which can be up to hundreds of feet long.

Light rays are in the middle of the spectrum. Thousands of light rays can be packed into 0.1 inch (2.5 mm).

The shortest rays are gamma rays, which have billions packed into 0.1 inch (2.5 mm).

▲ Very long waves are displayed on the left of the electromagnetic spectrum. Shorter waves are displayed to the right.

Capturing Image and Sound

In a television studio, a television camera lens captures images. The camera scans the images line by line and turns them into a signal. When all the lines have been scanned, the complete image has been captured. Systems in some countries scan 525 lines of light and others scan 625 lines. The scans are converted to picture signals.

A microphone captures sounds. The microphone changes the patterns of the sound waves into electrical signals that can be carried by radio waves.

camera tube

2. The colored light is displayed on a plate. A beam of electrons from the camera tube scans the pattern of light in lines.

1. A recorded image is divided into red, green, and blue light and passed through tubes, one for each color.

camera

prism splits the light

Transmitting Images Line by Line

In 1884, a German engineering student, Paul Nipkow, came up with the idea of cutting an image into separate lines and transmitting them line by line. This became the basis of the scanning technique used in transmitting television signals.

Cable and Internet Television

Not all television signals are broadcast through the air. Cable television stations deliver their signals straight into people's homes, through wires and cables. Internet television is delivered over an Internet connection to a television.

◀ An analog television camera scans images about 30 times a second. A digital television camera scans twice as many images each second, which makes a better quality picture.

Transmitting Signals Through the Air

The sound and image signals are then sent to **transmitters**. The signals are combined with radio waves so that they will travel through the air (see page 26). One transmitter sends the images and another sends the sound. The signals are picked up by a **receiver**.

▲ Television signals are picked up by a television antenna. Inside the television set, the signals are decoded and turned back into images and sound.

Word Watch

receiver something that receives signals
transmitters things that send signals

Web Watch ▼

www.sciencetech.technomuses.ca/english/collection/television.cfm
www.howstuffworks.com/tv.htm

How Do Cell Phones Work?

Cell phones are actually a form of radio. They broadcast their signals over radio frequencies. Every cell phone call is managed by a complex **network** of cells.

Sound Carried on Radio Waves

Sound waves can be carried as radio signals on radio waves (see page 24). A **transmitter** creates radio waves by creating electrical **pulses** at a certain **frequency**. The frequency is the number of radio waves that pass a point each second. It is measured in units called hertz (Hz), with one hertz equal to one wave per second. **Receivers** that are tuned into a particular frequency can decode the **sequences** of the pulses.

Cell phones have both transmitters and receivers. They are similar to walkie-talkies or two-way radios, but people using walkie-talkies must speak at different times, because only one frequency is used. Cell phones transmit and receive messages on slightly different radio frequencies, which means more than one person can talk at the same time.

Cell Networks

Cell phone coverage depends on a system of cells. Cells are small geographic areas that are served by base stations with towers. Any calls made within a cell are directed through the base station.

A base station can only handle a certain number of calls at once, so city areas need to use lots of very small cells and base stations may be only 1,640 feet (500 m) apart. Country areas have fewer cells and the cells may cover many square miles.

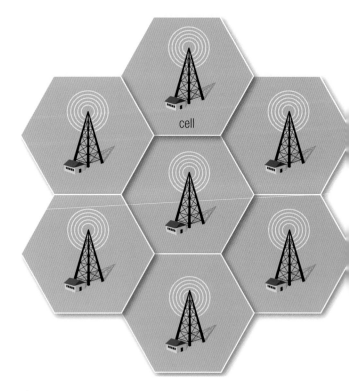

cell

▲ A cell is a hexagonal shape, which means it has six sides. Each cell has a number of frequencies that it can broadcast radio signals on. Cells that are beside each other cannot use the same frequencies, but cells that are not near each other can.

Word Watch

compresses presses together into a smaller space

frequency number of times something occurs in a given period

network group or system of things that are connected

pulses short bursts of a wave, with regular rhythm

receivers things that receive signals

sequences series of items that follow each other in a particular order

transmitter something that sends signals

Making and Receiving Calls

When a cell phone call is made, the cell base stations find the receiver and transmit the call.

1. When the caller dials a number, a signal goes from his or her phone to the base station of the cell within which the caller is located.

2. The signal arrives at the base station, the caller's details are identified, and the calling phone is assigned a frequency for the call. If all the frequencies are being used, the call will not proceed.

3. The signal is passed to the main telephone network. All different phone companies are connected to the telephone network.

caller

base station

main telephone network

receiver on cell phone

landline phone

4. The telephone network identifies the location of the intended receiver. If the receiver is on a landline, the signal is passed on directly. If the receiver is on a cell phone, the network identifies the base station closest to the receiver. The signal is then sent from the base station to the receiver at a vacant frequency.

5. If a caller or receiver starts moving toward the edge of a cell and into another cell, his or her signal will be transferred to the base station in the new cell. The frequency of the call will also change, but the caller and the receiver will not notice.

Cell Phones = Mobile Phones

The cell phone's name comes from the system of cells used to transmit its phone calls. Mobile phone is another name for a cell phone.

First Cell Phone Call

The first cell phone call across a cell system was made in a New York street on April 3, 1973, by Martin Cooper, a communications engineer for the company Motorola. Cooper is credited with inventing the first personal handset.

Web Watch ▼

electronics.howstuffworks.com/cell-phone.htm

Why Doesn't a Microwave Oven Get Hot?

A normal oven heats up food by heating the air around the food, but a microwave oven heats up only the food within the oven—not the air around it.

Microwaves and Molecules

Microwaves are a type of electromagnetic wave (see page 24). They are easily absorbed by water, fats, and sugars. Not all foods contain fats and sugars, but they do contain some water.

In a microwave oven, microwaves are produced by a **device** called a magnetron. When the microwaves hit water in the food, they cause the **molecules** in the water to turn one way and then another. This process continues as more and more microwaves hit the molecules. The twisting and turning movement creates heat and the heat cooks the food.

conventional oven

▲ Microwave ovens became cheaper and more popular in the late 1970s. They are now found in many kitchens.

microwave oven

▲ In a conventional oven, food is cooked from the outside in. In a microwave oven, food is cooked from the inside out.

Word Watch

device something made for a particular purpose or to do a particular job

molecules groups of atoms that are stuck together

Inside a Microwave Oven

All microwave ovens have the same basic features.

2. The microwaves shoot out in the form of a beam and across to a spinning fan. The fan reflects the waves toward the food in several directions.

1. When the microwave oven is turned on, microwaves are produced by the magnetron.

3. The walls and the metal grid on the door of the oven reflect microwaves back toward the food.

beam divider

fan

microwave beam

magnetron

4. The microwaves enter the food and produce heat energy in its water, fat, and sugars.

5. The turntable turns the food so that it cooks evenly.

▲ A microwave oven is well **insulated** to prevent the microwaves from leaking out.

Different Heating Times

Because water absorbs microwaves, food with high water content cooks quicker than food with less water. This is why it takes a shorter time to heat up a cup of soup than it does to heat a bowl of pasta.

Word Watch

insulated covered by materials that slow down the transfer of heat to or from an object

Web Watch ▼

home.howstuffworks.com/microwave.htm

Some technological advances and inventions come about after years of tests, trials, experiments, building, and rebuilding. On the other hand, some come about almost by accident. Liquid Paper® and Post-it® Notes are two such inventions.

Liquid Paper®

Liquid Paper® was invented in 1951 by typist Bette Graham, who wanted to avoid having to retype a whole page whenever she made a mistake. She got the idea after watching some painters repaint a spot where they had made mistakes. She went home and experimented with paint. It was a success.

▲ Liquid Paper® is the brand name of the first correction fluid.

How Correction Fluids Work

Correction fluids such as Liquid Paper® contain a material that can be applied as a wet liquid and which quickly sets. The correction fluid covers up the mistake because it is the same color as the piece of paper.

Correction fluids have five types of ingredients:

- ⊃ Solvents are substances that are capable of dissolving other substances. They are usually liquids.

- ⊃ Colorants are dyes or other matter that provide something with color.

- ⊃ Resins are solid substances that are obtained naturally from plants or created in laboratories. In correction fluids, the resin provides a base for the colorants.

- ⊃ Dispersants are chemicals that break up the colorants into smaller particles and help them spread out evenly.

- ⊃ Fragrances are added to correction fluids to stop people from inhaling the fumes.

The right combination of these ingredients creates a product that can be laid on thinly and dries quickly.

Famous son

Bette Graham's son Michael Nesmith was a member of one of the world's most successful pop bands, The Monkees.

Mistake Out!

Bette Graham originally called her invention Mistake Out.

Web Watch ▼

www.liquidpaper.com

Post-it® Notes

Post-it® Notes is the brand name for a type of stationery that has a sticky strip on the back. They were developed in the laboratories of the 3M scientific research company.

Developing the Idea for Post-it® Notes

In 1968, a scientist at 3M, Spencer Silver, developed a very low-adhesive glue. He was not deliberately trying to develop such a product, but he quickly recognized that it had some potential. The glue could be used to stick paper on certain surfaces, and the sticky note could be removed and reused. Few others shared Silver's excitement at his discovery.

In 1974, one of Silver's colleagues, Art Fry, realized that the adhesive would be perfect to use on a bookmark for his hymnbook. It would stop his bookmark from falling out while he was singing in church. Soon 3M saw some potential for the product and they launched Post-it® Notes in 1977.

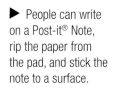

► People can write on a Post-it® Note, rip the paper from the pad, and stick the note to a surface.

▼ Art Fry is one of the inventors of Post-it® Notes.

Web Watch ▼

www.3m.com/us/office/postit
www.3m.com/us/office/postit/
pastpresent/history.html

Index